TASHA CHERRY

You Are that Tree (1)

Prayer and Workbook

Copyright © 2020 by Tasha Cherry

All rights reserved. No part of this publication may be reproduced, stored or transmitted in any form or by any means, electronic, mechanical, photocopying, recording, scanning, or otherwise without written permission from the publisher. It is illegal to copy this book, post it to a website, or distribute it by any other means without permission.

First edition

This book was professionally typeset on Reedsy. Find out more at reedsy.com

Contents

Prayer and Workbook	iv
CHAPTER 1	1
CHAPTER SUMMARY	2
CHAPTER TWO	7
CHAPTER SUMMARY	8
CHAPTER THREE	14
CHAPTER SUMMARY	15
CHAPTER FOUR	20
CHAPTER SUMMARY	21
CHAPTER FIVE	25
CHAPTER SUMMARY	26
CHAPTER SIX	33
CHAPTER SUMMARY	34
CHAPTER SEVEN	41
CHAPTER SUMMARY	42
CHAPTER EIGHT	49
CHAPTER SUMMARY	50
CHAPTER NINE	58
CHAPTER SUMMARY	59
CHAPTER TEN	68
CHAPTER SUMMARY	69
CHAPTER ELEVEN	74
CHAPTER SUMMARY	75
CHAPTER TWELVE	79
CHAPTER SUMMARY	80

Prayer and Workbook

CHAPTER 1

FOR HIS GLORY
*I saw a large tree in the middle of the earth. The tree grew very tall and strong, reaching high into the heavens for all the world to see. It had fresh green leaves, and **it was loaded with fruit for all to eat.** Wild animals lived in its shade, and birds nested in its branches. **All the world was fed from this tree.**"* **Daniel 4:10-12**

CHAPTER SUMMARY

God created each of the trees in the midst of the Garden for a specific purpose. And every description of the tree in the midst of the garden was meant to fit the ideal life God has designed for you to live. You were made to fulfill a specific purpose that brings glory to God.

Activity 1.0

Carefully read Daniel 4:1-22 and Genesis 2:15-17. Write down your thoughts on these verses.

....
....
....
....
....
....
....
....
....
....
....
....
....

Question 1.0

In what ways does Daniel's interpretation of Nebuchadnezzar's dream sound closely related to the tree in the Garden of Eden?

....
....
....
....
....
....
....
....
....
....
....
....
....

REASONING WITH THE WORD

Do you think God created each of the trees in the midst of the Garden for a specific purpose?

Tick one: **Yes**... **No**...

What is the reason for your answer?

....
....
....
....
....
....
....
....
....

Question 1.1

What might have been the consequence, if man had proceeded

to eat of the tree of life after the fall?

....

Activity 1.2
Read Daniel 4:10-12. Outline five main features of THE TREE described in the three verses of that Scripture.

....

Question 1.1
Explain how the features of this TREE relate to your life, business, Ministry, work, family, etc.? (*You may use your notebook*

CHAPTER SUMMARY

if the space isn't enough)

....
....
....
....
....
....
....
....
....
....
....
....

Life Assignment and Counsel

Begin to walk in the promises of God. Let your testimony challenge many to serve the Lord.

Live in a way that brings blessings to others. Do not just look like you have it. Exercise and walk in your authority.

Constantly see a picture of where God wants you to be. You see a picture of your next level.

Think, plan, act! Take your life, your business, your academic pursuit, your finances, etc., to the next level.

PRAYERS

O Lord, I don't just want to be addressed as 'King and Priest' or merely retain a title as 'Majesty,' please lead me back into the position of power and authority, in the Name of Jesus Christ. Amen!

Heavenly Father, please align my outward with my inner being.

Break all satanic attacks on my emotions, and life in general.

O God, let the kingship and blessings I declare begin to manifest in my life, in Jesus' Name. Amen!

DECLARATIONS

I declare that,

I am the large tree in the middle of the earth. I am 'a large tree' in the midst of my family, business, Ministry, work place, and in fact everything I do. I am not made for the low places of the earth. I occupy the central position, the peak of life. I am made for the topmost height. I am ABOVE ONLY!

I am tall and strong, reaching high into the heavens for all the world to see. I am in a blessed position that 'all the world' – everyone around me and beyond - can see what God is doing in and with my life.

My leaves are green and fresh and I am loaded with fruits for all to eat. My life brings tremendous blessings to others. My life provides shade to both friends and foes. Many live and find rest in my shade and nest in my branches.

My life fulfills God's specific purpose and brings glory to Him. I walk in the promises of God and my testimony shall challenge many to serve the Lord.

CHAPTER TWO

MOVE AWAY
Then answered Jesus and said unto them, Verily, verily, I say unto you, The Son can do nothing of himself, but what he seeth the Father do: for what things soever he doeth, these also doeth the Son likewise.
John 5:19

CHAPTER SUMMARY

In trying to move our lives to the next level, we have to begin to move away. God wants to help us see things differently. When we are with the people around us, we tend to see things from their perspective. But God wants us to take a step forward. He wants us to begin to see things from His own perspective. So, as long as we need to experience the next level, we must move away from the people around us for a time.

Activity 2.0

Read Mark 8:22-26. Write down your personal thoughts about the blind man's miracle.

....
....
....
....
....
....
....
....
....
....
....
....

CHAPTER SUMMARY

Question 2.0
Judging from the understanding in the main textbook, (1.) what does "the village: represent? (2.) Why did Jesus lead this man out of the village before praying for him?

....
....
....
....
....
....
....
....
....
....
....
....
....

Life Assignment and Counsel

Move away from the familiar to the Godly. Find out and write down what new steps you perceive God wants you to take, and take them.

Stop seeing from your perspective and that of those around you. If you want to move to the next level, step forward. Get the bigger picture for your life, business, children, family, job, etc. Don't be fixed in the old. Start thinking, and write down ways you can make things different around you, and make adequate plans to step up higher.

Move away from what you always know how to do, to what God wants you to do. Stop depending on the people around you and learn dependence on God. Let God become more real in your life. Learn how to seek Him and get answers. Don't just float around in your relationship with Him.

Question 2.1
From the sourcebook, what is the implication of spitting on a person's eyes or face?

....
....
....
....
....
....
....
....
....
....
....

Question 2.2
In few sentences, explain how "spitting in the eyes" relates to the Truth of God's Word and the change it can bring to your life.

....
....
....
....
....
....
....
....
....
....
....

REASONING WITH THE WORD

CHAPTER SUMMARY

"Most men are merely walking around as trees but have lost their authority." Do you agree with this statement?

Tick one: **Yes... No....**

Explain the reason for your answer below:

....
....
....
....
....
....
....
....
....

Question 2.3

What does God expect you to do as the tree in the midst of the garden? Why does He see you as the Tree of Life? In what ways does He expect you to establish the spiritual in the natural?

....
....
....
....
....
....
....
....
....
....
....
....

Question 2.4

What understanding do you need to establish, to move to the

next level? To take up the new position at your company? To go from working for someone else to working for yourself?

....
....
....
....
....
....
....
....

Question 2.5

What is the overall lesson you derive from the encounter of the blind man on your needed separation?

....
....
....
....
....
....
....
....
....

Life Assignment and Counsel

Separate yourself from some people around you for some time. There are people who do not encourage your growth in God; who do not challenge you to get out of your comfort zone. Move away from anyone who blurs your vision of God's realities for your life.

CHAPTER SUMMARY

Spend some days fasting and digging deeper into the Word of God in order to hear clearly what God has in mind for your life. Separation from men unto God will open your spirit to hear more clearly from the Spirit of God.

PRAYERS

Father please help me to see myself and the people around me clearly. Give me a clear vision of the people that I am surrounding myself with.

Grant me the grace and direction O Lord, to move away from people I'm tangled with. Help me to step forward and see things from Your perspective.

Lord please open my heart to trust more in You. Let every dependence on men be broken completely, in the Name of Jesus Christ.

I receive the grace to be humble in order to receive all that You have for me dear Lord.

I exercise authority over everything around me, and command that all what God has positioned for me in the spiritual, be made manifest in my life in the Name of Jesus.

DECLARATIONS

I declare that,
I see things from God's perspective.
I am totally dependent on God.
I am the tree of life. I ooze life and blessings to the people around me.
I am a commander of the blessing.

CHAPTER THREE

PUT GOD IN CHARGE
This is the interpretation, O king, and this is the decree of the most High, which is come upon my lord the king: That they shall drive thee from men, and thy dwelling shall be with the beasts of the field, and they shall make thee to eat grass as oxen, and they shall wet thee with the dew of heaven, and seven times shall pass over thee, **till thou know that the most High ruleth in the kingdom of men, and giveth it to whomsoever he will"** **Daniel 4:24-25**

CHAPTER SUMMARY

God wants to be the greatest influence over our lives. He wants to be the center of our lives. He wants to have first place. He wants to be in charge. He wants to be our first priority. He does not want us to make our decisions and then come ask Him to bless them. He wants to make the decisions and we are blessed when we choose between the tree of life and the tree of knowledge of good and evil, which are both within us.

Activity 3.1

Read Daniel 4:13,14. Write down your personal thoughts on the reasons why Nebuchadnezzar lost his place.

....
....
....
....
....
....
....
....
....
....
....
....

REASONING WITH THE WORD

A person can be a tree but his decisions can cost him his position.

True or False? ……………………………………

Give an example to explain your answer.

……………………………………………………………………………
……………………………………………………………………………
……………………………………………………………………………
……………………………………………………………………………
……………………………………………………………………………
……………………………………………………………………………
……………………………………………………………………………
……………………………………………………………………………
……………………………………………………………………………

Daniel 4:24-25 says, *"This is the interpretation, O king, and this is the decree of the most High, which is come upon my lord the king: That they shall drive thee from men, and thy dwelling shall be with the beasts of the field, and they shall make thee to eat grass as oxen, and they shall wet thee with the dew of heaven, and seven times shall pass over thee,* **till thou know that the most High ruleth in the kingdom of men, and giveth it to whomsoever he will***"*

Nebuchadnezzar gave the place or glory that was due God to himself and the result was drastic.

Question 3.1

List **FIVE BASIC WAYS** you can avoid Nebuchadnezzar's mistake:

……………………………………………………………………………
……………………………………………………………………………
……………………………………………………………………………
……………………………………………………………………………
……………………………………………………………………………

CHAPTER SUMMARY

....
....
....
....
....
....
....

Question 3.2
Mention and explain one major implication of walking out of God's Word or making wrong choices:

....
....
....
....
....
....
....
....
....

Question 3.3
What is the final result of making a wrong decision and moving further and further away from the Garden or position God placed you?

....
....
....
....
....
....
....
....

YOU ARE THAT TREE (1)

Life Assignment and Counsel

From now on, *choose to put God in charge of everything about your life, and see things from His perspective.* Always ask, what does God think about this?

Learn to prioritize God's Word. Let your decisions be based on what He says, not just what you think is right. That is the best recipe for acceleration to your next level. Do not make decisions based on emotions or sentiments. Always find out what the stand of God's Word is, and stand on that.

PRAYERS

Dear Lord open my eyes to Your pre-ordained plan of for my life. Help me to know what You created in the spirit so that I can begin to fully manifest it in the natural.

Holy Spirit, please help my decisions and utterances to keep in step with God's grace.

Lord I make up my mind to seek Your Face, to crave Your Voice, and to bow to You alone. I reject the voice of the serpent, and the curse of disobedience in my life, in Jesus' Name.

Father I invite You to be the CENTRE of my life, from beginning to the end. I command every other authority or influence over my life, broken in the Name of Jesus Christ.

DECLARATIONS

I declare that,

I am changing positions.

My life is not a tree full of leaves but without fruit. I am a fruitful blessing.

I give God all the glory for everything He does in my life.

CHAPTER SUMMARY

My God is the center of my life. He has first place in my life. God is in charge of my life. He is my first priority. I see things from His perspective.

CHAPTER FOUR

GOOD DECISIONS OR GODLY DECISIONS
So the man gave names to all the livestock the birds in the sky, and all the wild beast animals. But for Adam, **no suitable helper** *was found.* **Genesis 2:20**

CHAPTER SUMMARY

In order to move from one place or position to the next, we have to stop making good decisions and begin to make Godly decisions. We need to change our decisions in the direction of bringing honor to our King, the One Who died that we may live. And one of the areas we need to make adequate changes to honor God and move our life forward, is in the people we have around us. We need the right kind of people – suitable people around us.

Question 4.0

How do you differentiate between a good decision and a godly decision?

....
....
....
....
....
....
....
....
....
....

Activity 4.0

List out a few times or situations you think you may have asked for Barabbas in your life, family, business, etc.

....
....
....
....
....
....
....
....
....
....
....

Question 4.2
From the sourcebook, what do you think you can do now, if the same situations present again?

....
....
....
....
....
....
....
....
....
....
....

Question 4.3
Mention one area you need to make adequate changes to honor God and move your life forward. What is the major reason why some people keep taking one step forward and two

CHAPTER SUMMARY

steps backward in life?

....
....
....
....
....
....
....
....
....
....
....
....

Life Assignment and Counsel

Begin to make changes that will bring the needed progress in your life.

Take your place of authority. Start learning to recognize a Godly decision.

Sit down and pray about your business plan, the book that you want to write, the direction of your company, etc.

PRAYERS

Father please forgive me for all the times I have asked for Barabbas in my life? Lord please help me to always make a choice for You whenever I have to.

O God, help me to change my decisions with respect to the kind of people around me, and bring honor to You, in the Name of Jesus Christ.

Holy Spirit, please align my life with the most suitable people for the assignment you have for my life.

Open my eyes, O Lord, to see any changes I need to make that will bring the needed progress in my life.

Father I don't know what is best for my life, but You do. Take the lead O Lord, and help me to follow You.

DECLARATIONS

I declare that,

I make anointed, pre-ordained choices.

I decide to glorify God with my life.

My decisions bring honor to my King.

I align myself with suitable people in life.

I take my place of authority. I have the ability through God's Spirit, to recognize a Godly decision.

I am not a shadow of myself! I am the tree in the midst of the Garden, both in name and in authority.

CHAPTER FIVE

A STRUGGLE EXISTS
The babies jostled each other within her, and she said, "Why is this happening to me?" **Genesis 25:22,** NIV

CHAPTER SUMMARY

Man existed in God first, before he became existent on earth. We began to exist on earth when God formed and gave us a body. The soul is pre-existent, and has long existed before the body. The body only comes into the picture at birth. So, the soul is the older of the two. But we find that the body lords over the soul a lot of times. Nevertheless, the death of Christ was meant to bring both body and soul under the rule of ONE KING, which is Jesus Christ or God's Word.

Activity 5.0

Read Ecclesiastes 3:15, NLT. Write down your thoughts in relation to "the soul of man."

....
....
....
....
....
....
....
....
....
....

CHAPTER SUMMARY

REASONING WITH THE WORD

Man existed in God first before he became existent on earth. What do you think about this?

Tick one: **Yes, it's true... No, I don't think so... I'm not sure...**

Explain in Scriptural terms, the reason for your answer:

....
....
....
....
....
....
....
....
....
....
....

Question 5.0

From the sourcebook, what would you consider to be our major struggle, using Rebecca, Esau and Jacob, as examples?

....
....
....
....
....
....
....
....
....
....

Question 5.1

What are the *leaks and onions* in your life that make the struggle between body and soul real? What things are you addicted to?

Question 5.2

Explain how the coming of Christ to die for our sins was designed to bring change to the struggle between the body and the soul.

CHAPTER SUMMARY

....
....
....
....

Activity 5.1
Read Hebrews 4:12. Put down your thoughts on Paul's words in relation to Ezekiel's prophecy of ONE KING.

....
....
....
....
....
....
....
....
....
....
....

Question 5.3
How are the *Tree of Life* and the *Tree of the knowledge of good and evil* represented in our lives?

....
....
....
....
....
....
....
....
....

Question 5.4
What are the ultimate implications of both trees in our lives?

Question 5.5
From a very practical point of view, what would you say are the consequences of trying to make things happen our way, instead of waiting on God?

CHAPTER SUMMARY

....
....

Life Assignment and Counsel

Write down your greatest addictions and spend time with God in His Word and prayer concerning them. They may not be handled in one day, but like the walls of Jericho, they will certainly be broken.

Claim God's rule over your body and soul through the death of Christ.

Patiently wait on God to fulfill His promises in your life. Do not try to manipulate your way to anything to get anything.

PRAYERS

O Lord, I receive the grace to overcome double-mindedness.

I refuse the rule of my body over my soul in the Name of Jesus.

I command every addiction in my life broken by the power of the Holy Spirit.

By the death of Jesus Christ, I bring my body and soul under the rule of Christ and His Word.

I reject separation created by the tree of the knowledge of good and evil in my life.

Heavenly Father, I ask for forgiveness for all the times I have tried to manipulate my way to having what I want, in Jesus' Name.

DECLARATIONS

I declare that,

My body does not lord over my soul.

I am addicted to the Lord Jesus.

The Word of God has absolute impact and control on my soul.

My life expresses the fruits of the tree of life rather than the tree

YOU ARE THAT TREE (1)

of good and evil.

CHAPTER SIX

THE APPLE
And when the woman saw that the tree was good for food, and that it was pleasant to the eyes, and a tree to be desired to make one wise, ***she took of the fruit thereof, and did eat, and gave also unto her husband with her;*** *and he did eat.* **Genesis 3:6**

CHAPTER SUMMARY

Has God ever made you a promise and you tried to make it happen by your power? Have you ever gotten tired of waiting on God and decided that you were going to make something happen? But think about, God never said the promise would be born from something outside of you. He rather said the promise would come from within the center of you, *the tree of life*. That makes a world of difference.

Activity 6.0
Read Genesis 3:6. Write down your thoughts on the verse.

....
....
....
....
....
....
....
....
....
....
....

Question 6.0

CHAPTER SUMMARY

Metaphorically, what do you consider to be "The forbidden apple" presented in this chapter? Mention four people who partook of this apple to their detriment.

....
....
....
....
....
....
....
....
....
....
....
....

Activity 6.1

Carefully outline the major similarities in the operation of Eve, the wife of Adam, and Sarah, the wife of Abraham.

....
....
....
....
....
....
....
....
....
....
....
....

Activity 6.2

YOU ARE THAT TREE (1)

Give a detailed explanation of the chaotic result of Sarah's "apple."

....
....
....
....
....
....
....
....
....
....
....

Question 6.1

Has God ever made you a promise and you tried to make it happen by your power? Have you ever gotten tired of waiting on God and decided that you were going to make something happen? At such times what did you do?

....
....
....
....
....
....
....
....
....
....
....

CHAPTER SUMMARY

Question 6.2
What was the drastic result of the step you took? How would you handle the same event today?

....
....
....
....
....
....
....
....
....
....
....

REASONING WITH THE WORD
God had promised Rebecca that she would have two children, but the older shall serve the younger. Do you think God was going this Word to pass without Rebecca's interference?
Tick one: **Yes... No...**
Give reasons for your answer:
....
....
....
....
....
....
....
....
....
....

Activity 6.3

From the main textbook, explain what you consider to be Rebecca's biting the apple. Describe also the consequence of her helping Jacob steal his brother's birthright.

Question 6.3

In what ways did Jacob miss out on God's plans for his life?

CHAPTER SUMMARY

....

Life Assignment and Counsel

Find the "apples" in your life. Where have you tried to manipulate situations and circumstances to your advantage? Make a 360 degrees turn.

What mistakes did you make in teenage or youth days that affect your life today? Read Psalms 25:7. Wait upon the Lord and seek His mercies.

Take the time to think about your decisions before you make them. Asking yourself, *"What are the long-term effects from making this decision? Am I solving a problem or creating another?"*

PRAYERS

Father please help me to avoid the "The forbidden apple" like a plague.

Help me O God, never to present the forbidden apple to anyone in the course of my life.

Father help me to feed my faith by Your Word instead of my doubts, in the Name of Jesus. Teach me to wait upon You O God.

Forgive me O Lord for anything I tried to make happen outside of You.

Lord help me never to take anything that will separate me from what is rightfully mine, in the Name of Jesus Christ.

Dear Lord may I never miss You or Your plans for my life. Whatever of my flesh stands in the way of Your perfect plans for my life, may it be destroyed completely in Jesus' Name. Amen!

May the Blood of Jesus speak mercies concerning every mistake in my past that has planted the wrong tree, in the Name of Jesus Christ.

DECLARATIONS

YOU ARE THAT TREE (1)

I declare that,
I am a person of faith and absolute trust in God.
My faith in God's Word is firm.
God's promises will come to pass in my life.
I do not try to fulfill God's Word.
I possess only what is rightfully mine.
I cannot and will not miss out on God's plans for my life.
My fleshly desires do not dominate me.

CHAPTER SEVEN

WHAT SHOULD I EXPECT?
The creation waits in eager expectation for the sons of God to be revealed. **Romans 8:19-20**, NIV

CHAPTER SUMMARY

When God speaks, our question to Him should be, "What should we expect?" It should not be disbelief. It should not be that a part of us believes that God will do it, and another thinks He won't. We shouldn't laugh or scorn at His Word because we think God waits too long to get anything done. The simplest thing we should present before God is that we'd love to understand our role in the transaction: "Lord what should I expect in what you just told me?"

Activity 7.0

Outline a major difference between Eve's doubts and Mary's question to the Angel Gabriel.

………………………………………………………………………………
………………………………………………………………………………
………………………………………………………………………………
………………………………………………………………………………
………………………………………………………………………………
………………………………………………………………………………
………………………………………………………………………………
………………………………………………………………………………
………………………………………………………………………………
………………………………………………………………………………

CHAPTER SUMMARY

Activity 7.1
Outline also, a major difference between Mary's reaction to God's Word about her conception and Sarah's reaction to God's Word about her conception.

Question 7.0
What should be your response to God's Word when He says something about your life that is way beyond human possibility?

....
....
....
....
....
....
....
....
....
....
....

REASONING WITH THE WORD
Adam and Eve were already created in the image of God. They had authority on earth, so they were 'gods' in their own right.

True or False?............................

Explain your answer with at least two Scriptural backups.

Question 7.1
Describe a New Testament temptation that is akin to what the devil did with Eve in the Garden of Eden. What can you say is the difference between the two?

....

Question 7.2

In a short summary, how can you explain satan's "identity crisis" operation using the American slave trade era?

Question 7.3

Explain the statement, "Mary was different. She didn't give her husband the apple to bite at all. She left that where it was supposed to be – completely up to God."

CHAPTER SUMMARY

....
....
....
....
....
....
....
....
....
....
....
....

Question 7.4
When you find yourself in Mary's kind of situation, what should be your disposition?

....
....
....
....
....
....
....
....
....
....
....
....

Question 7.5
If you are considering connecting to a person, and you're wondering if they're the right one, what should you expect from God as a confirmation?

....

Question 7.6

What is the raw material in your life for the birthing of the supernatural? Explain.

Activity 7.2

Read Romans 8:19. Outline three things in your life, of which manifestation you can say the earth is awaiting.

CHAPTER SUMMARY

....
....
....
....
....
....
....
....
....
....
....

Life Assignment and Counsel

When God says something that appears bigger than what your mind can handle, get on your knees and ask Him, "Lord what should I expect?" Never laugh or scorn at God's Word. Carefully find out your role in His transaction with your life.

Always make the decision to obey God's Word, even if you don't have a clear understanding of where He is leading you.

Never try to convince people about something God is doing in your life. Leave it all in His hands.

If you are wondering if the other person is the right partner for you in marriage, business, etc., allow them to get a Word or revelation from God too. Don't try to convince them.

PRAYERS

Lord give me the grace to ponder at Your Word with faith rather that scorn in unbelief.

Heavenly Father, please help me to understand my role in Your transactions with my life.

I reject every satanic deception that is against God's calling for my life.

I come against anything that tries to separate me from my identity in order to access and overwhelm my mind with an evil suggestion, in the Name of Jesus.

O God, grant me the grace to leave everything about my life in Your hands, in Jesus' Name.

Dear Lord, help me to give birth to Your seed within me, and use it to bring change to my generation in the Name of Jesus Christ.

DECLARATIONS

I declare that,

I walk by faith and not by sight.

I celebrate God's Word and ideas for my life.

God's time is the best for me.

God has made me a god on earth. I have the authority to enforce God's will where I am.

I do not have identity crises. I know who I am in God.

I am not worried over what is God's business.

Creation is awaiting my manifestation.

I am giving birth to God's seed in my life.

CHAPTER EIGHT

DIVINE TIMING
Jesus saith unto her, Woman, what have I to do with thee? mine hour is not yet come. **John 2:1**

CHAPTER SUMMARY

There is a specific time for the accomplishment of every purpose. We must understand
Divine timing. God moves people. We don't! Understanding what part we play and what part God plays is a big part of the puzzle. There is a process in doing things. Sometimes we want to rush the process so we can get to our expected end, but there is always a revelation period. When we give God His place, everything else will fall in place.

Activity 8.0

Read Ecclesiastes 3:1, and John 2:1. Write down your thoughts on these Scriptures in relation to Divine timing.

....
....
....
....
....
....
....
....
....
....

CHAPTER SUMMARY

Question 8.0
How did David's understanding of Divine timing regulate his attitude?

Activity 8.1
"God moves people. You don't! Understanding what part you play and what part God plays is a big part of the puzzle." Explain this quote in your own words:

REASONING WITH THE WORD

"There is a bit of difference between being anointed and being appointed." Do you agree with this?

Tick one – **Yes I do... No I don't... I'm not sure...**

Give reasons for your answer, with Scriptural examples.

....
....
....
....
....
....
....
....
....
....
....

Activity 8.2

Give a vivid description in your own words, of the anointing and appointment of Jesus Christ, the Son of the Living God.

....
....
....
....
....
....
....
....
....
....
....

CHAPTER SUMMARY

Question 8.1
What is the importance of the Holy Spirit in the manifestation of God's calling for our lives?

Question 8.2
What was the role of God's unction in the appointment of Jesus?

Question 8.3

What was the significance of Jesus' visit to the Garden immediately after His resurrection?

....

....

....

....

....

....

....

....

....

....

....

....

Activity 8.3

Explain the best way to get your company, business, products, Ministry, etc., to the masses using an understanding of how God planned to reveal Christ to the world.

....

....

....

....

....

....

....

....

....

....

....

CHAPTER SUMMARY

Question 8.4

What is the danger of connecting people who aren't like-minded? People who don't bear God's anointing and testimony on their lives?

Question 8.5

What is the relation between the right relationship and the product of your conception?

Life Assignment and Counsel

Always wait for God's time.

Try to find out your part in God's move. Never force yourself into a position that isn't yours.

Read Isaiah 32:15. Seek the blessing of the Baptism in the Holy Spirit. Study on it. Read books. Pray until He comes on your life.

Spend time in prayer, asking God to restore your relationship with Him before you were born.

Let God to be the Head of your life, your marketing team, your Ministry, your network, your business, then all else will fall in place.

Look for people who are like-minded and get connected to them. Look for those who already bear God's anointing and testimony on their lives, not those who are trying to go about it on their own.

PRAYERS

Lord help me not to miss Your timing for the accomplishment of Divine purpose in my life.

Father deliver me from premature arrival in life. Open my eyes to see when my exposure to the masses must be.

Open the eyes of my heart Lord. Grant me the understanding of things that should be left to You alone to handle.

Dear Lord take me to the place of manifesting Your call on my life by pouring out Your Spirit upon me in full measure.

Restore O Lord Jesus, all my lost years in the journey of life, in the Name of Jesus Christ.

Heavenly Father, be the Head of my life, marketing team, Ministry, network, and business, in the Name of Jesus Christ.

Connect me O Lord to the right person and let my life take on a new dimension.

CHAPTER SUMMARY

I sever every connection to the wrong person in the Name of Jesus.

DECLARATIONS

I declare that,

I understand and operate in Divine timing.

I do not miss my time of visitation and accomplishment.

God is moving people to favor me.

I have the 'Seed of God' within me.

By the Spirit's descent I am entering into the fullness of Who I am supposed to be.

My life is receiving restoration my relationship with God before I was born.

God is the Head of my life. God is the strength of my life. God is the pillar of my destiny.

I am connected to the right people. I am birthing supernatural change.

CHAPTER NINE

SOUND OF THE TRUMPET
When the trumpets sounded, the people shouted, and at the sound of the trumpet, when the people gave a loud shout, the wall collapsed; so every man charged straight in, and they took the city. **Joshua 6:20**, NIV

CHAPTER SUMMARY

The seeds of God are His Words, His plans, His thoughts, His voice. And if we can recognize the seeds that are in our life, we can make change - real change - rather than just have the illusion or the shadow of change. We must recognize the differences between the seeds of God and the seeds of Satan in our lives. That will ultimately decide if we become the Tree of Life in the earth or the tree of good and evil.

Question 9.0

From the chapter summary above, what would you say are the seeds of God? What is the benefit of recognizing the difference between the seeds of God in our lives and that of satan?

....
....
....
....
....
....
....
....
....
....

Activity 9.0

Read Deuteronomy 1:2. Explain in your own words the reason you think an entire generation was prevented from entering the Promised Land.

....
....
....
....
....
....
....
....
....
....
....

Question 9.1

What seeds in your life are preventing you from receiving what God has promised you? Why aren't you moving forward in life? What lies have you believed that are preventing you from taking hold of God's promise? Think and enumerate them below:

....
....
....
....
....
....
....
....

CHAPTER SUMMARY

....
....
....
....

Question 9.2
Look at some common beliefs outlined in the sourcebook. What beliefs do you put over the Word of God in your own life? Write down any you can remember.

....
....
....
....
....
....
....
....
....
....
....

Question 9.3
How should you handle such beliefs in order to make meaningful progress in life?

....
....
....
....
....
....
....
....

REASONING WITH THE WORD

"What you believe affects the way you act."

True or False?..................

Give a Scriptural example to support your choice.

Question 9.4

The Israelites at the base of the mountain likened God's voice to a trumpet. How would you describe the trumpet in relation to God's Voice?

CHAPTER SUMMARY

....
....
....
....
....

Life Assignment and Counsel

Learn to recognize the seeds that are in your life in order to make real change, rather than just have the illusion or the shadow of change. Recognizing the differences between the seeds of God and the seeds of Satan in your life will ultimately decide if you become the Tree of Life in the earth or the tree of good and evil.

To move forward, you must believe the Precious Word of God instead of your own opinion.

What seeds in your life are preventing you from receiving what God has promised you? Why aren't you moving forward in life? What lies have you believed that are preventing you from taking hold of God's promise?

Discard every belief you put over the Word of God in your own life. You can't put anything above God's Word and make any meaningful progress in life.

Whose voice are you listening to? God's voice, your own voice or that of the snake in the Garden? To move forward with your life, try to recognize the voice of God.

Activity 9.1

Using Martin Luther King Jnr., describe what happens when the church gets in one accord.

....
....
....
....

Activity 9.2

Isaac said to Esau, *"You will live by the sword and you will serve your brother. But when you grow restless, you will throw his yoke from off your neck"* (Genesis 27:40, NIV). Enumerate the yokes on your life you would love to see broken.

....
....
....
....
....
....

In what ways do you intend to get rid of such yokes?

....
....
....
....
....
....

Question 9.6

From the sourcebook, how would you explain the concept of "day" with reference to 2 Peter 3:8?

....
....
....
....
....
....

Question 9.7

How does the Concept of Day explain the case of Joshua and

CHAPTER SUMMARY

the Israelites bringing down the walls of Jericho in seven days?

....
....
....
....

Activity 9.3

Read Joshua 5:13-15. Explain what took place before the walls of Jericho came crumbling down.

....
....
....
....
....
....

Question 9.8

What does it mean to "take off your shoes?"

....
....
....
....
....
....

Question 9.9

It is good not to give the apple a bite. But what happens if someone gave you the apple and unknowingly, like Adam, you bit it?

....
....
....
....
....

YOU ARE THAT TREE (1)

Life Assignment and Counsel

Sometimes God doesn't solve a particular problem through one generation but several. Just keep on with your prayers, your fasting, your intercession, etc. Soon, those walls will collapse at the sound of the trumpet.

Don't walk your path; walk the path that God has already pre-ordained. Renounce your own path. Find out and follow God's path.

ACKNOWLEDGE that God rules in your affairs. Take off your shoes and surrender to His path.

Trust God's choices for you instead of trying to force your way into relationships, friendships, companies, and businesses that God never meant for you to have.

Consider every decision you make. Always ask, is God in it or just me?

PRAYERS

I pray O God for the grace to recognize Your seeds in my life.

May my ears be opened to recognize the differences between Your seeds O God and the seeds of Satan in my life, that I may ultimately become the Tree of Life in the earth.

Heavenly Father, open my eyes to see the seeds in my life that are preventing me from receiving what You have promised me.

Lord I discard every belief that I have put over Your Word in time past.

Let every stubborn situation in my life be conquered eventually by the power of Your Word.

Father I take off my sandals. I choose to walk your path instead of mine in the Name of Jesus Christ.

CHAPTER SUMMARY

DECLARATIONS

I declare that,
I am not double-minded. I do not birth duality.
I am the Tree of Life in the earth.
I belong to the blessed generation.
I carry good report.
I will never stop my journey half-way
I am moving my life forward.
I break out of every undue yoke over my life.
Walls are crumbling around me.
My destiny is opening up.
I am birthing supernatural things.

CHAPTER TEN

SNAKES AND ANGELS
*She is **a tree of life** to those who embrace her; those who lay hold of her will be blessed.* **Proverbs 3:18** (NIV)

CHAPTER SUMMARY

As we see in Jesus' Ministry, Peter had given a revelation of Who Jesus was. Jesus stated clearly that Peter was speaking by the revelation of His Father in heaven. A few moments later, Peter said something else, and Jesus calls him Satan. Jesus knew that the enemy was speaking through Peter at that point. So, He was actually addressing the voice that spoke through Peter and not Peter as a person. From this, it becomes clear that we are exposed to two major influences or voices from which we have to choose.

Activity 10.0

Using the main textbook, compare and contrast the temptation of Jesus and that of Judas. What do you learn from the way Judas ended?

……………………………………………………………………………
……………………………………………………………………………
……………………………………………………………………………
……………………………………………………………………………
……………………………………………………………………………
……………………………………………………………………………

Question 10.0

What was the sole objective of Jesus' fast?

……………………………………………………………………………

Activity 10.1

Read Matthew 16:22-23. Write down your thoughts on this passage.

....
....
....
....
....
....

Question 10.1

Peter was trying to save Jesus. He was trying to protect Jesus. Why did Jesus address him as satan in the process?

....
....
....
....
....
....

Question 10.2

Just a moment earlier, Peter had given a revelation of Who Jesus was. Jesus said His Father gave Peter the revelation of Who He is. A few moments later, He called Peter Satan. What does this say to you?

....
....
....

CHAPTER SUMMARY

....
....
....

Activity 10.2
Read MY STORY in the main text. Outline the key features and lessons you have from the story.

....
....
....
....
....
....
....
....
....
....
....
....

Question 10.3
How would you explain the challenge of putting the snakes out of my garden in terms of putting calories out of my diet?

....
....
....
....
....
....

Question 10.4
What happens if you only do a little bit of dieting and then get back to eating your normal way? What happens if you put away the snakes and return to the things you did before?

....
....
....
....
....
....

Life Assignment and Counsel

Take out time to wait upon the Lord as you are led, in order to get leadership direction; and to know the will of God.

Counter satanic temptations with God's Word. And don't stop countering them.

Screen every suggestion concerning your life's assignment, no matter the source. Peter spoke from God and then from the devil in a short split of time.

Don't turn around to the things you left behind.

PRAYERS

Father Your Word says, with thee is the fountain of life, and in thy light we see light. Lord grant me direction in this journey of life. Help me to see light in your light. Help me to know Your will, in the Name of Jesus Christ.

Grant me the wisdom and grace Dear Lord to overcome every obstacle on my way to knowing Your will and purpose for my life.

I pray for the sensitivity to differentiate between Your Voice and the voice of the serpent, even from fellow brethren, in the Name of Jesus.

Grant O Lord, the grace never to return to my vomit or permit the snakes again in my life, in the Name of Jesus Christ.

DECLARATIONS

CHAPTER SUMMARY

I declare that,
I stand. I will not fall. I cannot fall. I choose to stand.
I receive direction from above. I walk in the will of God.
I am focused on my Master. No power of hell can misplace, misguide, or break my focus.
I am my shepherd's sheep, and I hear His Voice.
I am trained and disciplined for exploits in the kingdom.

CHAPTER ELEVEN

IDENTIFYING VOICES
When I was a child, I talked like a child, I thought like a child, I reasoned like a child. When I became a man, I put childish ways behind me. 1Corinthians 13:11, NIV

CHAPTER SUMMARY

The first struggle many have is how to know the difference between the voice of the snake and that of the angel. They think the angel only speaks good and the snake only speaks evil. But it's important to understand that sometimes the VOICE we believe to be of the enemy is not necessarily the voice of Satan; it is sometimes the voice of God. The voice of God does not always bring the GOOD news we want. Sometimes the voice of God prepares us for what is coming ahead. It is like the person who gives weather forecast. He tells us what to expect.

Activity 11.0

Read 1 Corinthians 13:11. What are your thoughts on that verse of Scripture?

....
....
....
....
....
....

REASONING WITH THE WORD

"We all have questions that we want God's input, and we all want to know His answers. But the reality is, God is never silent." Do you agree with this?

Tick one – **Yes... No...**
Give a possible reason for your answer.

Question 11.0
From the main textbook, what is the FIRST SOLUTION Jesus offers to identifying the voices?

....

Question 11.1
What is the SECOND SOLUTION Jesus offers to identifying the voices?

....
....
....
....
....
....

Question 11.2
What unspoken word does our fast have towards God? How does God respond to this?

....
....
....
....
....
....

Question 11.3
In relation to the spirit, what is the effect of denying the flesh certain pleasures, especially food?

....
....
....
....

CHAPTER SUMMARY

....
....

Activity 11.1
Read the story of the loss of my son, Timothy. What do you think about asking God for what will satisfy you, even when it's outside His will?
....
....
....
....
....
....

REASONING WITH THE WORD
"Sometimes the VOICE we believe to be of the enemy is not necessarily the voice of Satan; it is sometimes the voice of God."
True or False?..........................
Give Scriptural reasons for your answer.
....
....
....
....
....
....

Life Assignment and Counsel
Determine to know the difference between the voice of the snake and that of the angel. Do not take NO for an answer.

Make demands on God's input on whatever He wants you to do. Make demands on His input on your job, life partner, dwelling place, etc. Find out what His mind is on everything you want to do. You will never lose, if you do this always!

Be a person of prayer. Do not be a fickle, nominal Christian.
Practice the art of fasting and prayer, and make it a lifestyle.
Do not just "ask" from God. Find out if it is His will for you. Sometimes, simply pray, "Your will be done."

PRAYERS

Lord please teach me to know the difference between the voice of the snake and that of the angel.

Father please show me what You want me to do on every aspect of my life.

Help me Dear Lord to separate my will from Your will. Renew my strength as I spend intimate time with You.

From today Lord, I take off my shoes: "Not my will, but Thine be done."

DECLARATIONS

I declare that,
I am a child of God. My ears are opened to the Voice of my Savior.
The snakes are out of my ways by the power of God's Word.
I seek God's input in every inch of my life.
I am a person of prayer. I pray as I breathe; I breathe as I pray.
I pray in line with the will of God always.
I do not pray to get my way, but His will alone.

CHAPTER TWELVE

IT'S ALL ABOUT HIS WILL
What is happening now has happened before, and what will happen in the future has happened before... Ecclesiastes 3:15 (NLT)

CHAPTER SUMMARY

We are living in the now, but the future has already happened. It means we've already decided things in the spirit realm. That decision has already been made in creation. We simply have to bring the decision into time. The inward conflict we have in the midst of a decision is a sign that we're stuck struggling between two choices. One choice is the tree of life, and the other is the tree of good and evil. There is no in-between.

Activity 12.0

Read Ecclesiastes 3:15 (NLT). Write down your thoughts about this Scripture.

....
....
....
....

Activity 12.1

Based on your understanding of the main textbook, explain the statement, "We were in the creative process together with God."

....
....
....
....

CHAPTER SUMMARY

Activity 12.2

Read the first few paragraphs of the sourcebook. Explain in your own words the sentence, "We are pregnant with a solution for mankind."

....
....
....
....
....
....
....
....

Question 12.0

Using the concept of inward conflict, how do you know that God has made a decision about a matter?

....
....
....
....
....
....
....
....

Question 12.1

With reference to Jesus' agony, how can you best explain a replay of the Garden of Eden at the Garden of Gethsemane?

....
....
....
....
....

REASONING WITH THE WORD

"The inner conflict you experience is not about the choice; it is about you trying to get your way. The reason why you're conflicted is because you don't like His choice." Do you agree with this?

Tick one – **Yes, I do.... No, I don't**

Explain the reasons for your choice below:

....
....
....
....

Question 12.2

Jacob got his way with God, but walked with a limp the rest of his life. What lesson does this hold for you?

....
....
....
....

Activity 12.3

Take a seat in a calm environment. Write down all your needs and greatest desires right now. Take a look at them all and ask yourself, how many of these are not just about me but about God and His plans for my life?

....
....
....
....
....

CHAPTER SUMMARY

....
....
....

Question 12.3
Now look inwards. What's is your focus? Are you focusing on protecting yourself rather than focusing on the work that needs to be done?

....
....
....
....

Question 12.4
What are you conflicted about right now? What struggle is going on in your inward man about something in your life? List them below:

....
....
....
....

Question 12.5
What do you think God is saying in that situation?

....
....
....
....

Life Assignment
Teach your flesh to carry out what you've already decided in God. We're living in the now, but the future has already happened. Learn how to bring your eternal decisions into time by constantly making declarations.

You are pregnant with a solution for your generation. Discover it!

Kill your will! Sometimes that means you must not try to save your life, or protect yourself. You must get rid of all the 'what if's'.

Satan wants you to focus on saving yourself, promoting yourself, and making yourself important. No! Focus on the work that needs to be done in the Kingdom, not just protecting yourself.

Always focus on the bigger picture! You can overcome your fears, your innate ability to want to save yourself and instead, sacrifice your life and your will for His plan.

Pay attention to the labels on the products you consume for knowledge and wisdom. Pay attention to the options in your life, so you could exercise your faith.

PRAYERS

Lord I want to be Your servant, giving all I have to You, giving all I have to please You more. So help me Lord.

I command my flesh to carry out the eternal decisions that pertain to my life, in the Name of Jesus.

Father, by my declarations, I bring all my eternal decisions into time, in Jesus' Name.

I command the channels of my spirit to open up. Whatever solution I am pregnant with for my generation, I command it to come to manifestation.

Father it's not about me, but all about Your will and plan for my life. I dissolve every inner conflict or struggle by giving way to Your will alone, in the Name of Jesus Christ.

DECLARATIONS

I declare that,

I am a partner with God in creation.

My flesh obeys and carries out eternal decisions.

I am connected to God.

I am pregnant with a solution for mankind.

I am addicted to the will of God.

CHAPTER SUMMARY

My flesh is subject to my spirit.
I am focused on God's Kingdom work.
I am a light in someone's life.
I see the big picture.
I am the tree of life.

CONCLUDING ASSESSMENT

What is the meaning behind the tree of life?

....
....
....
....

What is the purpose of the other tree in the midst of the Garden - the tree of the knowledge of good and evil?

....
....
....
....

What does this mean to our lives?

....
....
....
....
....
....
....

www.ingramcontent.com/pod-product-compliance
Lightning Source LLC
Chambersburg PA
CBHW052118110526
44592CB00013B/1659